cooking with
grey goose vodka

GREY GOOSE
— VODKA —

DISTILLED AND BOTTLED
IN
FRANCE

40% ALCOHOL BY VOLUME. (80 PROOF) 750 ML

IMPORTED

cooking with
grey goose vodka
recipes by chef pascal courtin

Sidney Frank Importing Co., Inc.

TEHABI BOOKS

TEHABI BOOKS produced *Cooking with Grey Goose Vodka* and has developed and published many award-winning books that are recognized for their strong literary and visual content. Tehabi works with national and international publishers, corporations, institutions, and nonprofit groups to identify, develop, and implement comprehensive publishing programs. Tehabi Books is located in San Diego, California.
www.tehabi.com

President: Chris Capen
Sales Director: Eric Pinkham
Director, Trade Relations: Marty Remmell
Art Director: Vicky Vaughn
Editor: Terry Spohn
Production Artist: Mark Santos
Proofreader: Lisa Wolff
Indexer: Ken DellaPenta

For information, please write: Tehabi Books, 4920 Carroll Canyon Road, Suite 200, San Diego, CA 92121.

Sidney Frank Importing Co., Inc.

Sidney Frank Importing Co., Inc., was founded in 1972 to turn import specialty liquor items into national brands. www.sidneyfrankco.com

Photography: Michael Smith, Eddie Berman
Design: Bill Henderson, Michael Bond, Jack Egan, iDesign
Food Stylist: Susan Draudt
Writer: Aaron Crecy, Deirdre Maher

Reader inquiries should be directed to Sarah Zeiler of Sidney Frank Importing Co., Inc.
Email: szeiler@sidneyfrankco.com

Grey Goose® L'Orange. Orange flavored vodka./Grey Goose® La Vanille. French vanilla flavored vodka./Grey Goose® Vodka. Distilled from grain./Grey Goose® Le Citron. Lemon flavored vodka. 40% Alc./Vol. Imported by Sidney Frank Importing Co., Inc. New Rochelle, NY 10801.
Please Drink Responsibly.

ISBN 1-931688-06-0

Printed through Dai Nippon Printing Co., Ltd., in Korea

GREY GOOSE *L'Orange*   GREY GOOSE *La Vanille*   GREY GOOSE —VODKA—   GREY GOOSE *Le Citron*

foreword by sidney frank   It's no secret; I love food. From when I was a boy growing up on a farm, to my years spent overseas during World War II, to my time spent traveling throughout the world on business, there is nothing I enjoy more than sitting down to a fine meal.

Knowing full well that the best way to enjoy good food is with good drink, I went into the liquor business. I started my own business in 1972, and since then, I have preoccupied myself with the mission of finding the best spirits the world has to offer and introducing them to the United States. I've been fortunate in that many of the brands I've brought to the United States, including Grey Goose Vodka, have become successes. I've also been fortunate because, while searching for these gems around the globe, I've had the pleasure of sampling some of the finest cuisine the world can dish up.

Food says so much about the people who prepare it. They pour their creativity and passion into every dish, seasoning each with a bit of their background. I've always been somewhat awe-struck by chefs, and when I meet an exceptional one, I am truly impressed. A few years ago, I met someone who I believe to be one of the finest chefs of our time. I didn't have to take out my passport and travel to another continent. In fact, all I had to do was visit a nearby pastry shop in Westchester, New York. There, I tasted the creamiest crème caramel, sumptuous chocolate soufflés and sublime chocolate madeleines. The chef's name was Pascal Courtin, and I immediately asked him to come work with me as my personal chef. To my great happiness, Pascal agreed, and my gratitude and waistline have been growing ever since.

Schooled in France, Pascal brings culinary tradition and

innovative imagination to my kitchen. Delighted by all his creations for more than three years, I decided to put Pascal to a true test. I asked Pascal to come up with recipes using Grey Goose Vodka, the vodka I created in 1997 and which subsequently has been named the world's best tasting vodka. Grey Goose Vodka is one of the fastest growing brands in liquor history, but can you create an entire menu with it? As it turns out, you can, and a fantastic menu at that. From elegant

appetizers to decadent desserts, Pascal has created an unparalleled collection of vodka-based recipes. Indeed, the best way to enjoy good food is with good drink, and so it is my pleasure to share this collection of Grey Goose Vodka inspired recipes with you.

Cheers!

Sidney Frank

introduction by chef pascal courtin   Raised in the famed Bordeaux region of southwestern France, I enjoyed a decidedly enviable childhood in an idyllic setting. Home to many of the country's oldest and finest vineyards, the area's fertile soil has given birth to some of the world's most celebrated red wines. But it was not winemaking that ultimately captured my fancy; rather, it was another of the province's great passions — cooking.

My grandmother owned a quaint, country-style restaurant in Savignac, where I spent many an hour visiting. I recall helping her prepare crêpes for a Mardi Gras celebration at the age of 10, carefully measuring the ingredients and mixing the batter with a large wooden spoon. Afterward, we wrapped a crêpe in aluminum foil and placed it on the top shelf of the pantry, an ancient tradition believed to bring happiness to the household.

A warm-hearted woman with an easy smile and an infectious laugh, my grandmother was a loving culinary mentor — her early tutelage regarding the intricacies of cakes, crêpes, croissants and tarts provided a formidable foundation for my subsequent training as a pastry chef.

My grandmother often discussed the importance of

chef
pascal
courtin

culinary relationships, emphasizing the delicate balance of flavor, texture and even color when selecting ingredients. In particular, she introduced me to the art of cooking with wine—a vital undertaking when one lives in the heart of the world's most storied appellation. One day, I brought her a fresh lamprey from the nearby Garonne River; before my eyes, she used red wine and leeks to transform the fish into a gourmet feast.

Like my grandmother, I often experiment with wine and other spirits when cooking. As a result, I embraced the opportunity to create a cookbook incorporating the flavors of Grey Goose. Distinguished by their purity and panache, the four flavors of Grey Goose Vodka—Original, L'Orange, Le Citron and La Vanille—impart an assortment of unduplicated tastes.

My intention is to provide a departure from tradition—a collection of simple recipes with exquisite taste and uncommon visual appeal. Accordingly, you will find that I have used Grey Goose along with an assortment of new ingredients and garnishes to inspire a broad spectrum of original and classic cuisine.

I extend my deepest gratitude to Sidney Frank, whose delicious Grey Goose Vodkas serve as the cornerstone for this cookbook. He has been a gracious and generous patron from our first meeting, a chance encounter at a New York *pâtisserie* early on a Sunday morning in the fall of 1999. A few weeks later, Mr. Frank invited me to become his personal chef, an opportunity that has extraordinarily affected my life in both personal and professional capacities.

It is my intention that the following recipes capture Mr. Frank's buoyant disposition—he is an affable man who desires to unite the world with laughter, kindness and a dash of Grey Goose for good measure!

May this cookbook contribute an air of festivity to your every occasion.

Bon appétit,

Pascal Courtin

cocktails

grey goose vodka
classic martini

3 ounces of Grey Goose
 Vodka
 a whisper of vermouth

Shake with ice, strain, and serve
with an olive or lemon twist.

black tie martini

3 ounces of Grey Goose
Vodka
1/4 ounce of scotch
1/4 ounce of Campari®

Shake with ice, strain, and serve
with a pearl onion on a toothpick
nestled between two black olives.

grey goose l'orange
cosmopolitan

3 ounces of Grey Goose
L'Orange
$\frac{1}{2}$ ounce of Cointreau® or
Grand Marnier®
dash of cranberry juice
squeeze of fresh lime

Shake with ice, strain, and
garnish with lime peel.

citron martini

3 ounces of Grey Goose
Le Citron

Garnish with a twist of lemon.

grey goose le citron

apple martini

3 ounces of Grey Goose
     Le Citron
     dash of Cointreau®
     dash of Pucker® Sour Apple
     Schnapps

Shake with ice, strain, and
garnish with a slice of Granny
Smith Apple.

grey goose le citron

blue goose

2 ounces of Grey Goose
   Le Citron
1 ounce Hpnotiq® Liqueur
3 ounces white cranberry
   juice

Shake with ice and strain into an
ice-filled tumbler. Garnish with a
Swedish Fish candy.

vanilla martini

3 ounces of Grey Goose
    La Vanille

Shake with ice, strain, and
garnish with three coffee beans.

grey goose la vanille
chocatini

2½ ounces of Grey Goose
La Vanille
1 ounce white créme de cacao

Coat rim of martini glass with
chocolate syrup. Shake with ice
and strain.

appetizers

ingredients

- 4 potatoes, shredded, not rinsed
- 1 pound crab meat
  - salt to taste
  - freshly ground pepper to taste
- 1 bunch cilantro, chopped
- 1/2 teaspoon Worcestershire sauce
- 1 tablespoon Grey Goose Le Citron
  - flour
- 4 tablespoons butter or sunflower oil

sauce

- 1 cup mayonnaise
- 1/2 teaspoon Worcestershire sauce
- 1 tablespoon Grey Goose Le Citron
  - parsley, chopped

This richly flavored delicacy can be either an appetizer or an entrée. Grey Goose Le Citron sauce is an ideal accompaniment to the crab cakes.

grey goose le citron
crab cake

Preparation

Gently mix the potatoes, crab meat, salt, pepper, cilantro, Worcestershire sauce, and Grey Goose Le Citron. Shape the mixture into 3 inch flat patties and dredge in the flour. In a frying pan over medium heat, melt the butter or oil. Fry the patties on each side until golden in color. Drain on paper towels.

Sauce

To prepare the sauce, mix all ingredients in a bowl. Cover and refrigerate until ready to use. To serve, place two or three warm crab cakes on each plate. Serve with Grey Goose Le Citron sauce and sprinkle with parsley.

Serves 8

Named after a fifteenth-century Italian artist, carpaccio is a unique, lightly seasoned delicacy. Pascal adds faint nuances of basil, sugar, and Grey Goose Vodka, often serving it on toasted Italian bread.

ingredients

1 10-ounce filet mignon, frozen
parmesan cheese, finely sliced

sauce
50 leaves of basil
1 shallot
1 cup extra virgin olive oil
1 tablespoon sugar
salt
pepper to taste
2 tablespoons Grey Goose Vodka

grey goose vodka
beef carpaccio

Preparation
One hour before, thinly slice the frozen beef using an electric meat slicer. Place the slices of beef in a single layer in a circle on a serving plate. Place the parmesan slices in the center. Cover with plastic wrap and refrigerate until ready to serve.

Sauce
Place ingredients in a food processor and purée until smooth. To serve, drizzle with sauce and garnish with basil.

Serves 4

ingredients

24 blue point oysters
$1/2$ cup red wine vinegar
3 shallots, finely chopped
6 tablespoons Grey Goose Vodka
   salt
   freshly ground pepper
1 lemon, sliced
   small sprigs of parsley

This dish lends itself well to dinner parties and festive gatherings. Serve with a Grey Goose Le Citron martini for the perfect complement to the raw oysters.

grey goose vodka

blue point oysters

Oysters
Using the back edge of an oyster knife, pry open the shells (the shells can also be opened at your local fish market). Keep on ice.

Sauce
In a bowl, combine the red wine vinegar, shallots, Grey Goose Vodka, salt, and pepper. Divide the vinegar sauce evenly among 4 small cups. Place the cups in the center of 4 serving plates. Arrange 6 oysters on each plate. Garnish with a slice of lemon and parsley.

Serves 4

This super-chunky appetizer is the perfect precursor to a Mexican-style meal. The light citrus flavor of Grey Goose L'Orange reduces the intensity of the jalapeño peppers and adds a sweet finish.

ingredients

2 yellow bell peppers
4 large tomatoes, finely diced
½ orange bell pepper, finely diced
½ yellow bell pepper, finely diced
1 sweet onion, finely diced
½ cucumber, finely diced
2 garlic cloves, finely chopped

1 jalapeño pepper, finely minced
juice of 1 lime
3 tablespoons Grey Goose L'Orange
2 tablespoons cilantro, chopped
salt to taste
freshly ground pepper to taste

grey goose l'orange
california salsa

Preparation
To make a serving dish, cut ⅓ off one side of each of the 2 yellow bell peppers. Remove the seeds and set aside. In a mixing bowl, combine the remaining ingredients and mix well. To serve, spoon the salsa into yellow bell peppers.

Serves 4

ingredients

1 small Cavaillon melon or
  cantaloupe
  Grey Goose L'Orange

Equally suited as an appetizer or a dessert, the beauty of this refreshing dish lies in its simplicity. Quick and easy to prepare, it is perfect for the lazy days of summer.

grey goose l'orange
melon bowl

Preparation
Remove the top third of the melon and cut along the bottom to create an even standing surface. Scoop the seeds from the heart of the melon and fill with Grey Goose L'Orange. Refrigerate until cold and serve.

Serves 1

A seductive French delicacy, this salmon is a robustly flavored appetizer. Together with a measure of Grey Goose Vodka, soy, and cayenne pepper, the avocado-based purée gives the salmon a California flair.

ingredients

4   avocados
1   tablespoon extra virgin
    olive oil
    salt to taste
    freshly ground pepper
    to taste
    juice of 1 lime
1   pound fresh salmon filet
    salmon caviar

dressing

    juice of 1 lime
1   pinch cayenne pepper
2   shallots, finely chopped
1   garlic clove, finely chopped
2   tablespoons Grey Goose
    Vodka
1   teaspoon soy sauce

grey goose vodka
salmon tartare

Preparation
In a food processor, purée the avocado, olive oil, salt, pepper and juice of the lime. Dice the salmon filet and refrigerate until ready to use.

Dressing
To prepare the dressing, combine the juice of the lime, cayenne pepper, shallots, garlic, Grey Goose Vodka and soy sauce.

To serve, spoon the avocado purée into 4 martini glasses. Top with diced salmon and dressing. Garnish with salmon caviar.

Serves 4

ingredients

- 1 pound large sea scallops, rinsed
- 1/2 cup fresh lime juice
- 1 tomato, finely diced
- 1/2 yellow bell pepper, finely diced
- 1/2 orange bell pepper, finely diced
- 1 jalapeño, finely diced
- 1/2 red onion, finely diced
- 1/4 cup Grey Goose Le Citron
- 1/4 cup extra virgin olive oil
- 1 tablespoon cilantro, chopped
- salt to taste
- freshly ground pepper to taste
- sprigs of fresh cilantro for garnish

Sidney Frank fell in love with this hors d'oeuvre while summering in Curacao. Highlighted by subtle undertones of Grey Goose Le Citron, it draws raves from dinner guests.

grey goose le citron
scallop ceviche

Preparation

Slice each scallop horizontally into 3 or 4 thin pieces. Place the scallops and lime juice in a glass bowl and marinate for at least 5 minutes. In a large glass bowl, combine the remaining ingredients except the cilantro sprigs, and mix well. Add the scallops and lime juice. Refrigerate for at least 1 hour before serving. To serve, spoon the mixture into scallop shells. Garnish with fresh cilantro.

Serves 6

This scintillating shrimp cocktail is overflowing with an assortment of seasonings such as hot pepper sauce, horseradish and black pepper.

ingredients

20 jumbo shrimp
3 cups hot water
  salt to taste
5 coriander seeds
4 peppercorns
5 sprigs of fresh parsley
1 bay leaf
  juice of 1 small lemon
  chive sprigs for garnish
  limes, thinly sliced,
    for garnish

cocktail sauce

2 cups ketchup
3 tablespoons Grey Goose
    Vodka
2 tablespoons prepared
    horseradish
$\frac{1}{2}$ teaspoon salt
$\frac{1}{2}$ teaspoon ground black
    pepper
  juice of 1 small lemon
  hot pepper sauce to taste
  Worcestershire sauce to
    taste

grey goose vodka

shrimp cocktail

Preparation

Peel and de-vein the shrimp. Leaving the tails on, set the shells aside. Combine the shells, hot water, and salt in a medium saucepan; bring to a boil. Reduce heat to low, cover, and simmer until fragrant, about 20 minutes. Strain the stock through a sieve, pressing on the shells to extract all the liquid. Bring stock and remaining ingredients, except the shrimp and garnish, to a boil in a 3- or 4-quart saucepan for 2 minutes. Turn off heat and stir in shrimp. Cover and let stand for about 8-10 minutes, or until the shrimp are firm and pink. Drain shrimp, reserving stock for another use if desired. Plunge shrimp into ice water to cool, then drain. Serve shrimp chilled with cocktail sauce and garnish with chive sprigs and lime slices.

Cocktail Sauce

Mix all ingredients. Refrigerate the sauce until ready to use.

Serves 4

ingredients

spread

1½ cups sour cream
   salt to taste
   white pepper to taste
3 tablespoons Grey Goose
   Vodka
1 teaspoon fresh lemon juice

garnish

4 ounces thinly sliced smoked
   salmon, rolled
1 sweet onion, finely chopped
1 fresh basil sprig for garnish
   Beluga caviar

blini

⅓ cup warm water
1 package active dry yeast
¾ cup all-purpose flour
1 teaspoon sugar
2 egg yolks
¼ teaspoon salt
½ cup whole milk
3 tablespoons melted butter
2 egg whites

grey goose vodka

smoked salmon blini

Spread

In a bowl, mix the sour cream, salt, pepper, and Grey Goose Vodka. Add lemon juice to taste. Cover the bowl with plastic wrap and set aside.

Blini

In a small bowl, combine the water and yeast. Let stand for 10 minutes or until the mixture begins to foam. In a medium-sized bowl, combine the flour, sugar, egg yolks, salt, milk, butter, and yeast mixture and stir to form a smooth batter. Cover the batter with a damp towel and let rise at room temperature for 1½ hours.

Whip the egg whites until peaks form. Using a rubber spatula, gently and thoroughly fold the egg whites into the risen batter. Heat a griddle or heavy skillet over medium-high heat until hot, or until a few drops of water sizzle on the surface. Lightly grease the griddle. For each pancake, pour about 2 tablespoons of batter onto the griddle. Cook over medium heat for about 30 to 45 seconds, or until many bubbles appear on the surface. Before turning the blini, lift the edges to check that the undersides are golden brown. Turn the blini and cook for 20 to 30 seconds more, or until the undersides are golden brown. Transfer the blini to a baking sheet, cover loosely with foil and keep warm in the oven. Repeat with the remaining batter. Transfer the blini to a serving platter and top each one with a spoonful of the spread.

Garnish

Add the rolled smoked salmon, chopped onions, and caviar. Garnish with fresh basil.

Serves 8

Much of the fun in preparing this dish is selecting the fresh vegetables—I recommend organically grown produce. An elegant hors d'oeuvre, it features a Mediterranean sauce with feta cheese, anise, and Grey Goose Vodka.

grey goose vodka

grey goose vodka
vegetable tart

ingredients

12 red and yellow cherry tomatoes
6 baby zucchini, sliced
1 small eggplant, diced
1 red pepper, diced
1 yellow pepper, diced
1 green pepper, diced
6 red and yellow fine peppers
2 garlic cloves, chopped
2 tablespoons olive oil
  salt
  freshly ground pepper
10 ounces feta cheese
1 teaspoon anise seeds, crushed
3 tablespoons Grey Goose Vodka
1 bunch basil, chopped

pastry
1 cup flour
6 tablespoons unsalted butter, diced
1 pinch salt
$1/4$ cup water

Preparation

Preheat oven to 400°F. To prepare the pastry dough, combine the flour, butter, and salt. Mix with a fork or pastry blender until butter is combined with flour. Slowly add enough water to make a smooth dough. Grease six 3-inch tart pans with removable bottoms. Roll out the dough and cut into six 5-inch circles. Line each tart pan with dough and trim the edges. Prick the bottom of each pan several times with a fork. Bake in preheated oven for 10 minutes or until golden; set aside. Place all the vegetables on a parchment-lined baking sheet. Mix the garlic, olive oil, salt, and pepper; brush on vegetables. Roast the vegetables for about 30 minutes or until cooked. In a bowl, mix the feta cheese, anise seeds, Grey Goose Vodka, and half the basil until smooth. Divide cheese mixture evenly into tart pans and bake for 10 minutes. Remove from oven and top with roasted vegetables. Bake 10 minutes longer. Sprinkle remaining basil and ground pepper on warm tarts just before serving.

Serves 6

ingredients

- 4 tablespoons unsalted butter
- 1 small papaya, peeled, seeded, and sliced
- 1 mango, peeled and sliced
- 2 Macintosh apples, cored and sliced
  - juice of 1 lemon
- 1 cup seedless green grapes
- 1 foie gras, sliced ½-inch thick
  - salt to taste
  - freshly ground pepper to taste

sauce

- 1 cup water
- 1 cup sugar
- 6 tablespoons Grey Goose Le Citron

Sautéed papaya, mango, apples, and green grapes produce a colorful foie gras ripe with fruit flavors. With a measure of Grey Goose Le Citron, the sauce adds a sweet finish to the velvety dish.

grey goose le citron

foie gras

Preparation

In a large sauté pan over medium-high heat, melt half of the butter. Sauté the sliced papaya and mango until golden-brown, remove from the pan and reserve. In a large bowl, mix the apple slices with the lemon juice to prevent a discoloration. In the same sauté pan, melt the remaining butter and sauté the apples until golden; remove from the pan and set aside. Sauté the grapes for 1 minute. Sauté half of the foie gras floured over medium-high heat until golden, turn and sauté the other side. Remove the foie gras, drain on paper towel and reserve; save the fat in a jar for cooking. Proceed the same way for the remaining foie gras. Place the foie gras on 4 serving plates, season with salt and pepper and garnish with sautéed fruits and sauce.

Sauce

In a saucepan, bring the water and sugar to a boil over medium-high heat. Boil for 45 seconds until the syrup is clear. Stir to make sure all the sugar has dissolved. Add the Grey Goose Le Citron and remove from the heat.

Serves 4

55

soups & salads

Simple to prepare, this is an elegant soup that beautifully accents any meal. Served cold, the creamy yogurt-cucumber base has a velvet texture and subtle but distinctive taste.

ingredients

4 hot-house cucumbers, peeled
32 ounces plain yogurt
6 tablespoons Grey Goose Vodka
salt to taste
freshly ground pepper to taste
chives

grey goose vodka
cucumber soup

Preparation

Cut 3 cucumbers in half lengthwise and remove the seeds. Chop into cubes andpurée in a food processor or blender. Add the yogurt, Grey Goose Vodka, salt, and pepper. Blend until smooth. Refrigerate for 2 hours.

To serve, pour the soup into 8 stemmed cocktail glasses. Finely slice the fourth cucumber and arrange on top of the soup with the chive sprigs.

Serves 8

ingredients

- 2 tablespoons white wine vinegar
- 3 tablespoons Grey Goose La Vanille
- salt to taste
- freshly ground pepper to taste
- $^1/_2$ cup walnut oil
- 6 Belgian endives
- 4 ounces Roquefort, crumbled

Quick and easy to prepare, this light salad has sweet overtones. Use Grey Goose La Vanille to soften the sharp taste of the Roquefort and vinegar dressing.

grey goose la vanille
endive salad

Preparation

In a small bowl, mix the vinegar, Grey Goose La Vanille, salt and pepper together. Add the oil and mix until blended. Take off the larger outside leaves from each of the endives and arrange around the rim of 6 attractive cups. Place the smaller leaves inside, to look like a flower. Spoon the Roquefort into the center of the endives and refrigerate. To serve, whisk the Grey Goose La Vanille dressing and spoon it on each salad.

Serves 6

Use a variety of greens to achieve a myriad of tastes and colors. Grey Goose L'Orange, honey, and balsamic vinegar make the dressing a sweet and refreshing accompaniment.

ingredients

mixed greens
French white beans, cooked
parmesan cheese, finely
  sliced

dressing

8 tablespoons extra virgin
  olive oil
2 tablespoons balsamic
  vinegar
1 tablespoon honey
2 tablespoons Grey Goose
  L'Orange
  salt to taste
  freshly ground pepper
  to taste

grey goose l'orange

summer mixed greens

Preparation
Mix dressing ingredients well.
When ready to serve, toss the
greens with dressing, lightly
coating each of the greens.
Garnish with beans and slices of
parmesan cheese.

62   Serves 4

ingredients

- 1 pound roma tomatoes, peeled, seeded, and diced
- 1 garlic clove
- 3 cups tomato juice
- 1/4 cup Grey Goose Vodka
- salt to taste
- freshly ground pepper to taste
- hot pepper sauce
- 1 yellow pepper, seeded, and diced
- 1 orange pepper, seeded, and diced
- 1 green pepper, seeded, and diced
- 1 hot-house cucumber, peeled and diced
- 1 sweet onion, peeled and diced
- croutons
- parsley, chopped

This refreshing gazpacho arouses the taste buds with a fiery combination of Grey Goose Vodka, fresh peppers, hot pepper sauce, ground black pepper and onions. Served chilled for the consummate contrast.

grey goose vodka

gazpacho

Preparation

In a food processor or blender, purée the tomatoes and garlic. Pour into a large bowl. Add the tomato juice, Grey Goose Vodka, salt, pepper, and hot pepper sauce to taste. Mix in the peppers, cucumber, and onion. Refrigerate until well chilled. Serve in a martini glass topped with croutons and parsley.

Serves 4

This exotic dish was inspired by a trip to the Greek Isles. Brilliantly hued, it is a lightly seasoned salad that is perfect as a side dish or the main course.

ingredients

salad
- 4 sweet red peppers
- 4 sweet orange peppers
- 24 cherry tomatoes, red and yellow
- 1/2 pound fresh buffalo mozzarella, sliced
- basil

tapenade
- 5 ounces pitted black olives
- 4 tablespoons olive oil
- salt to taste
- freshly ground pepper to taste

dressing
- 8 tablespoons hazelnut oil
- 1 tablespoon apple cider vinegar
- 1 tablespoon honey
- 1 teaspoon dijon mustard
- 1 teaspoon finely chopped garlic
- 2 tablespoons Grey Goose Vodka
- salt to taste
- freshly ground pepper to taste

grey goose vodka

mediterranean salad

Preparation
Roast the peppers at 475°F until the skins are blackened. Place the heated peppers in a paper bag and close. Let sit for 15 minutes; remove the skin and seeds. To serve, arrange the peppers with the halved tomatoes and mozzarella on a plate with the tapenade. Drizzle with dressing.

Tapenade
Mix all the ingredients in a food processor and purée until smooth.

Dressing
Mix all the ingredients in a food processor until smooth.

Serves 4

ingredients

1   pound dried green
     split peas
3   russet potatoes
8   cups vegetable broth
¼   cup Grey Goose Vodka
½   cup heavy cream
     salt to taste
     freshly ground pepper
       to taste
     croutons
     chopped chives for garnish

Providing a pleasant respite from the winter chill, this hearty soup combines Grey Goose Vodka, potatoes, and split peas for a distinguished texture and a sharp finish.

grey goose vodka

split pea soup

Preparation

Rinse split peas. Place the peas, potatoes, and vegetable broth in a large saucepan. Cover and bring to a boil. Reduce the heat to medium and simmer for about 1 hour or until the peas and potatoes are tender. Purée the soup in a blender or food processor until smooth.

Stir in Grey Goose Vodka, heavy cream, salt and pepper. If the soup is too thick, thin it with more vegetable broth. To serve, ladle the soup into bowls and top each with croutons and chives.

Serves 6

Equally appropriate for either lunch or dinner, this nearly effortless dish tingles with the sharp flavors of fresh citrus and herbs. The Grey Goose Le Citron adds a sweet touch of citrus.

ingredients

1 pound white fresh
  mushrooms
  juice of ½ lemon
1 bunch of salad greens

sauce

7 ounces crème fraîche
  juice of ½ lime
1 bunch parsley, chopped
¼ teaspoon allspice
1 pinch ginger powder
2 tablespoons Grey Goose
  Le Citron
  salt to taste
  freshly ground pepper
  to taste

grey goose le citron

mushroom salad

Preparation

Wash the mushrooms, dry them with a paper towel and slice them lengthwise. Pour the lemon juice on the mushrooms and mix well so that they do not blacken.

Sauce

In a bowl, mix the crème fraîche, lime juice, parsley, spices, Grey Goose Le Citron, salt and pepper. Pour the Grey Goose Le Citron cream on the mushrooms and mix well. Transfer the salad to a serving platter, and garnish with the salad greens. Refrigerate until ready to serve.

Serves 4

entrées à la carte

If available, use Atlantic salmon. It is typically farm-raised and quite tender. Accented with Grey Goose L'Orange, cream, and orange juice, the dill sauce transforms this salmon filet into a masterpiece.

ingredients

4   ¼-pound Atlantic
    salmon filets
extra virgin olive oil
salt to taste
freshly ground pepper
    to taste

dill sauce
8   ounces rich fish stock,
    frozen
6   tablespoons Grey Goose
    L'Orange
2   cups heavy cream
1   bunch dill, chopped
    juice of ½ orange
    salt to taste
    freshly ground pepper
        to taste
    sprigs of dill for garnish

grey goose l'orange

atlantic salmon

Preparation
Preheat oven to 400°F. Place the salmon filets on a baking sheet lined with parchment paper. Brush the filets with olive oil and sprinkle with salt and pepper. Bake for 15 minutes, or until done.

Sauce
The dill sauce should be prepared at the last minute so the dill doesn't lose its flavor. In a saucepan, add the fish stock and Grey Goose L'Orange; reduce by half. Pour in the cream and heat slowly until the sauce thickens. Combine the sauce, dill, and orange juice in a blender and blend until smooth. Add salt and pepper to taste. To serve, place each filet on a plate and top with Grey Goose L'Orange dill sauce. Garnish with a dill sprig.

Serves 4

ingredients

- 1 tablespoon extra virgin olive oil
- 4 swordfish steaks
- 3 mangoes, peeled
- 2 tablespoons unsalted butter
- $^1/_2$ cup honey
- $^1/_4$ cup Grey Goose La Vanille

Inspired by the fresh, sweet mangoes found in the outdoor markets of Antigua, this sauce is a lovely complement to the rich, tender swordfish.

grey goose la vanille

caribbean swordfish

Preparation

In a sauté pan, heat oil to medium-high temperature. Sauté swordfish steaks for 10 minutes or until done; set aside. In a food processor, purée 2 mangoes until smooth. In a saucepan, cook the remaining mango, diced with the butter over low-medium heat for 5 minutes. Pour in the mango purée, honey and Grey Goose La Vanille and cook for 10 minutes more. To serve, place the fish on each plate and pour Grey Goose La Vanille mango sauce on the side. For garnish, steam red, yellow and green peppers and rice.

Serves 4

With a light, flaky texture, the
Dover sole is complemented by
a sauce laden with Grey Goose
Le Citron, shallots, and
crème fraîche.

ingredients

3 tablespoons unsalted butter
½ cup flour
4 Dover sole, cleaned and
   skin removed (by your
   fish market)
salt to taste
freshly ground pepper
   to taste

sauce
2 tablespoons unsalted butter
3 shallots, finely chopped
10 ounces Grey Goose
   Le Citron
10 ounces rich fish stock
   (frozen)
13 ounces crème fraîche
salt to taste
freshly ground white pepper
   to taste

garnish
4 lemon peel twists
   baby yellow squash,
   steamed
   brussels sprouts, steamed
   cherry tomatoes, cut in half

grey goose le citron
dover sole

Preparation
Melt the butter in a non-stick
frying pan on medium-high heat.
Lightly flour each fish. Sauté the
floured Dover sole on each side
until light golden in color. Set
aside, but keep warm.

Sauce
To make the sauce, melt the
butter in a saucepan over
medium heat. Add the shallots
and sauté until soft. Pour in
Grey Goose Le Citron and stir.
Boil the liquid until reduced by
half. Add the fish stock and boil
until reduced by one-third. Stir in
the crème fraîche, reduce the
heat to low-medium and cook
until the sauce thickens. Strain
the sauce, add seasoning to taste
and pour over the Dover sole.

Garnish
Garnish with a twist of lemon
peel and serve with steamed
vegetables and fresh cherry
tomatoes.

Serves 4

ingredients

- 1 tablespoon light olive oil
- 1 tablespoon garlic, chopped
- 1 onion, chopped
- 1 cup Grey Goose Vodka
- ½ cup brown sugar
- 1 teaspoon powdered mustard
  salt to taste
- ½ cup distilled vinegar
- ¼ cup Worcestershire sauce
- 2 cups ketchup
- ⅓ cup tomato paste
  cherry tomatoes, quartered,
    for garnish
- 4 T-bone steaks

Invigorated by Grey Goose Vodka and Worcestershire, this entrée is superlative for outdoor grilling. Grey Goose Vodka with a splash of tonic is the perfect counterpart.

country t-bone

Preparation

In a large skillet, heat the olive oil until warm. Add the garlic and onion; sauté until golden. Add Grey Goose Vodka, sugar, mustard, and salt; mix well. Add the vinegar, Worcestershire sauce, ketchup, and tomato paste, and bring to a boil. Reduce the heat to medium-low and simmer for 30 minutes. Strain sauce. Grill steaks to your liking, garnish with sauce and sliced cherry tomatoes and serve.

Serves 4

Distinguished by its sweet, citrus-flavored sauce, this dish is a wonderful entrée for a winter meal. Featuring Grey Goose L'Orange, the warm glaze enlivens both the duck and the fruit garnish.

ingredients

1 duck (about 5 pounds)
2 tablespoons vegetable oil
salt to taste
freshly ground pepper
   to taste

sauce

2 tablespoons butter
3 tablespoons flour
1^1/$_2$ ounces glace de canard
1^1/$_2$ cups water
2 tablespoons sugar
1^1/$_2$ cups fresh orange juice
3 tablespoons Grey Goose
   L'Orange
salt to taste
freshly ground pepper
   to taste

candied orange peel

1 cup sugar
1 cup water
   peel of 3 oranges, thinly
   sliced

garnish

3 oranges, peeled and sliced
2 mangoes, peeled and sliced
4 bananas, cut in half and
   sliced
4 slices of pineapple
^{1}/$_4$ cup unsalted butter
^{1}/$_2$ cup candied orange peel

grey goose l'orange

duck à l'orange

Preparation

Preheat oven to 475°F. To prepare the duck for roasting: cut off the wing tips, remove the fat from the tail section and truss the duck. Put the duck, oiled, salted, and peppered, in a non-stick roasting pan. Place in the oven on lower rack and reduce heat to 425°F. Cook for 1 hour and 20 minutes. Turn the duck and prick with a fork to allow fat to drain during cooking.

Sauce

In a small pan, melt the butter, over medium heat. Stir in the flour and cook for 1 minute. Mix in the glace de canard (see definition, page 126. You can find this in a gourmet store.); as a substitute, use concentrated chicken stock dissolved in water. Stir in the sugar and orange juice. Pour in Grey Goose L'Orange, add salt and pepper to taste and cook for 1 minute.

Garnish

For candied orange peel, combine the sugar and water in a small saucepan; bring to a boil until lightly thickened. Place the orange peel in the pan and boil for about 15 minutes, until soft. These can be stored in a plastic bag and refrigerated to be used on other desserts. Sauté each fruit, except orange peel, in butter until golden brown.

To serve

Place the duck on the platter, garnish with sautéed fruit and candied orange peel. Pour a few tablespoons of sauce over the duck and serve the rest in a bowl.

Serves 4

ingredients

1 pound fresh fettuccine
  salt to taste
  freshly ground pepper
    to taste
1 white truffle, sliced for
    garnish
  freshly grated romano
    cheese

sauce

½ cup chicken broth
1 white truffle, chopped
2 egg yolks
1½ cups heavy cream
4 tablespoons Grey Goose
    Vodka

The pride of Alba, Italy—home to the National Truffle Museum— white truffles are characterized by their earthy essence. This pasta features a cream-based sauce made with Grey Goose Vodka for an exceptional taste and silky texture.

grey goose vodka
truffle fettuccine

Sauce

In a saucepan, bring the chicken broth to a boil, add the chopped truffle and cook for 5 minutes on low heat. In a bowl, beat the egg yolks with the heavy cream. Stir the cream mixture and Grey Goose Vodka into the hot chicken broth.

Preparation

Cook the fettuccine al dente (see definition page 126) and drain. Toss sauce mixture with the hot pasta. Add salt and pepper to taste. To serve, divide pasta between 4 plates. Top each with truffle slices and grated romano cheese.

Serves 4

85

This dish features an abundance of fruit flavors. Made with Grey Goose Vodka and fresh cranberries, the sauce is an excellent counterbalance to the satiny chestnut purée.

ingredients

- 2¹/₂ pounds guinea hen
- 3 oranges, cut in half (remove pulp and reserve shell for garnish)
- ¹/₂ pound chestnuts, canned
  salt to taste
  freshly ground pepper to taste
  vegetable oil

chestnut purée
- 1 cup whole milk
- ¹/₄ cup sugar
- 1 pinch nutmeg
- ¹/₂ pound chestnuts, canned

sauce
- 4 cups fresh cranberries
- 1 cup water
- ¹/₂ cup sugar
- 3 tablespoons Grey Goose Vodka
  freshly ground pepper to taste

grey goose vodka
guinea hen

Preparation
Preheat oven to 425°F. In a bowl, combine oil, salt, pepper and chestnuts; stuff in the guinea. Roast for 1 hour. To keep moist, occasionally sprinkle water on the hen while cooking.

Chestnut purée
In a pan, place the remaining chestnuts, milk, and sugar and cook for 10 minutes. Add nutmeg and pepper. Place in a food processor and purée until smooth. Set aside.

Sauce
Place the cranberries and water in a saucepan. Cover and cook over medium heat until soft. Add the sugar, Grey Goose Vodka, and pepper and cook for 1 minute over medium heat. To serve, fill the orange halves with chestnut purée. Remove guinea from the oven, and cut into 6 pieces. Place them on a serving dish, along with whole chestnuts and orange cups stuffed with chestnut purée. Top the guinea with Grey Goose Vodka cranberry sauce.

Serves 6

ingredients

- 1 chicken, cut in 6 pieces
- 2 cups basmati rice
- 6 tomatoes, oiled and sugared
- parsley, chopped
- sprig of tarragon

sauce

- 2 shallots, chopped
- 1 tablespoon extra virgin olive oil
- 2 garlic cloves, chopped
- 1 cup chicken broth
- 1 teaspoon paprika
- 1 teaspoon Herbs de Provence, crushed
- 1 tablespoon cornstarch
- 1/4 cup water
- juice of 1 lemon
- 1/4 cup Grey Goose Le Citron
- 1/2 cup heavy cream
- 1 tablespoon dijon mustard
- salt to taste
- freshly ground pepper to taste

This main course is covered in a creamy sauce that features fresh herbs, spices, and Grey Goose Le Citron. It is a gourmet interpretation of Marian Frank's family recipe.

grey goose le citron

lemon chicken

Sauce

In a large pan, sauté the shallots in olive oil until golden. Add the garlic, chicken broth, paprika and Herbs de Provence, and mix well. Add the cornstarch, water, and lemon juice and cook until sauce thickens. At this time, pour in Grey Goose Le Citron, heavy cream, dijon mustard, salt, and pepper and cook for 10 minutes over low heat.

Preparation

Place the pieces of chicken in the sauce and cook for 45 minutes. To cook rice, bring 4 cups of water to a boil, add rice and simmer, covered, for 15 minutes. Cut the tomatoes in half and coat with oil and sugar. Broil the tomatoes until lightly browned. To serve, place the rice on a plate and arrange chicken on top with tomatoes; pour sauce over dish. Garnish with parsley and tarragon sprig.

Serves 6

This savory dish is ideal for the holidays. The combination of green grapes, sage, and Grey Goose La Vanille adds a sweet finish to the quail.

ingredients

- 2 tablespoons vegetable oil
- 8 quail
- $1/3$ cup Grey Goose La Vanille
- $1^{1/2}$ cups chicken stock
- 1 sprig fresh sage, finely chopped
- 2 cups seedless green grapes
- 1 sprig fresh sage for garnish

grey goose la vanille

quail

Preparation

Heat the oil in a deep frying pan and cook the quail on all sides until evenly browned. Add Grey Goose La Vanille and cook for 1 minute. Add the chicken stock, sage, and grapes. Cover the pan and simmer until the quail are completely cooked, about 10 minutes. Remove the quail and grapes and keep them warm. Bring the sauce to a boil; reduce by two-thirds or until syrupy. Strain the sauce and pour over the quail and grapes to serve. Garnish with sprig of sage.

Serves 4

ingredients

1 rack of lamb
  salt to taste
  freshly ground pepper
    to taste

sauce

1 cup plum jam
1/3 cup Grey Goose Vodka
  salt to taste
  freshly ground pepper
    to taste

An unpretentious yet elegant entrée, this dish is ideal for an intimate dinner party. Grey Goose Vodka and plum jam make a marvelous accompaniment to the lamb.

grey goose vodka

rack of lamb

Preparation
Preheat oven to 425°F. Salt and pepper the lamb. Brown lamb on both sides in a large frying pan. Place in preheated oven and roast for 25 to 30 minutes.

Sauce
Place all ingredients in a food processor or blender and purée. Simmer the sauce for about 10 minutes. To serve, combine lamb and sauce with stewed sweet petite corn and summer squash.

Serves 4

Grey Goose L'Orange combines with chanterelles, butter, heavy cream, and glace de viande in this twist on a classic.

ingredients

- 3 tablespoons butter
- 4 veal chops
  salt to taste
  freshly ground pepper
    to taste

sauce

- $^1/_4$ pound fresh chanterelles, diced
- 2 shallots, chopped
- $^1/_4$ cup Grey Goose L'Orange
- $^1/_2$ cup beef broth
- 1 teaspoon glace de viande
- $^1/_2$ cup heavy cream

garnish

- 1 tablespoon butter
- 1 teaspoon chopped garlic
- $^1/_2$ pound fresh chanterelles
  chopped parsley

grey goose l'orange
veal à la forestière

Preparation

In a large skillet, melt the butter over medium-high heat. Add the veal chops and cook until lightly browned on each side, about 10 minutes total. Season with salt and pepper. Transfer the veal to a serving platter and keep warm.

Sauce

Add the diced chanterelles to the pan and sauté about 2 minutes. Add the shallots and cook for 20 seconds. Add Grey Goose L'Orange and cook until the liquid is reduced by half, about 1 minute. Stir in the beef broth, glace de viande, and heavy cream and bring the mixture to a boil. Taste and adjust the seasoning if necessary. Mix the sauce in a blender until smooth.

Garnish

In a pan, heat the butter over high heat and sauté the garlic. Add the chanterelles and cook for 4 minutes. Stir in parsley. To serve, pour the sauce over the veal, add garnish and top with parsley.

Serves 4

desserts

Sweeten this apple dessert

with a delicious combination of

Grey Goose Vodka and cinnamon.

Served with Grey Goose

La Vanille ice cream, the

tarts are perfect for an

autumn evening.

ingredients

- 2 tablespoons flour
- 1 puff pastry sheet
- 4 large Golden Delicious apples
- 2 tablespoons unsalted butter, melted
- 2 tablespoons raw sugar
- 1 teaspoon cinnamon powder
- 2 tablespoons Grey Goose Vodka

grey goose vodka
apple tart

Preparation

Preheat oven to 400°F. Sprinkle flour on a rolling surface to keep the puff pastry from sticking. Roll the pastry out into a 12-inch square. Cut out four 6-inch circles. Place circles on a baking sheet covered with parchment paper. Slice the apples lengthwise into thin slices. Arrange apple slices in a concentric pattern on the pastry. Brush with the melted butter. Sprinkle with the sugar and cinnamon. Bake in preheated oven for 30 minutes. Sprinkle Grey Goose Vodka on the warm tarts out of the oven. Serve warm or at room temperature topped with Grey Goose La Vanille ice cream (see page 118).

Serves 4

ingredients

- 2 cups graham cracker crumbs
- $^1/_2$ cup melted unsalted butter
- $^3/_8$ ounce unflavored gelatin (1$^1/_2$ small packages)
- $^1/_2$ cup cold water
- 24 ounces cream cheese
- 1$^1/_4$ cups sugar
- 5 ounces evaporated milk
- 4 tablespoons fresh squeezed orange juice, strained
- $^1/_4$ cup Grey Goose L'Orange
- $^3/_4$ cup heavy whipping cream
- 1 orange, peeled and sectioned

sauce

- 5 oranges, peeled and sectioned
- $^1/_2$ cup sugar
- $^1/_4$ cup Grey Goose L'Orange

Flavored with Grey Goose L'Orange, this delightful dessert is a satiny blend of cream cheese and orange juice with a graham cracker crust. Try it with Grey Goose Le Citron for a slightly tart finish.

grey goose l'orange
cheesecake

Preparation

Preheat oven to 350°F. In a small bowl, mix the graham cracker crumbs and melted butter. Put the mixture in a 9-inch springform pan and press into the bottom and sides of the dish. Bake in the oven for 15 minutes and chill. In a small pan, sprinkle the gelatin over the cold water and let stand for 1 minute. Stir over low heat until the gelatin is dissolved and set aside. In a large bowl, beat the cream cheese and sugar until fluffy. Add the milk and orange juice; beat again. Scrape the bottom of the bowl to make sure there are no lumps. Add Grey Goose L'Orange to the gelatin mixture and blend well. In a medium bowl, whip the heavy cream, then add in cream cheese mixture. Pour filling into chilled crust and refrigerate for 8 hours before serving. Prepare the orange sections as garnish for the top of the cheesecake.

Sauce

Place the oranges and sugar in a food processor and purée. In a saucepan, bring orange purée to a boil. Reduce heat and simmer for 10 minutes. Add Grey Goose L'Orange and simmer for 5 minutes more. Strain the sauce and refrigerate. When serving, drizzle the sauce over individual cheesecake slices.

Serves 10

This decidedly French dessert was inspired by a trip to Cognac. The addition of Grey Goose L'Orange adds citrus highlights to the rich chocolate pastry.

ingredients

crème anglaise

- 2 cups whole milk
- 1 vanilla bean, cut in half
- 3 egg yolks
- 4 tablespoons sugar
- 2 tablespoons Grey Goose La Vanille

chocolate marquis

- 8 tablespoons unsalted butter
- 4 ounces dark chocolate
- 2 tablespoons Grey Goose L'Orange
- 2 eggs
- 4 tablespoons sugar
- 2 tablespoons flour
  powdered sugar

grey goose l'orange
chocolate marquis

Crème anglaise

Combine the milk and vanilla bean in a small saucepan. Slowly bring to a boil, then remove from heat, cover, and let sit for 10 minutes. Remove the vanilla bean. Beat the egg yolks and sugar until completely mixed. While beating, pour in the hot milk mixture. Place over low heat and cook until the mixture coats the back of a spoon. Set aside. Stir in Grey Goose La Vanille. Cool by placing in the refrigerator.

Chocolate marquis

Preheat the oven to 400°F. Melt the butter and chocolate in the microwave or bain-marie. Stir in Grey Goose L'Orange and let cool to room temperature. In a separate bowl, beat the eggs and sugar until slightly thickened and light yellow in color. Add the flour and mix well. Stir in chocolate mixture. Butter and flour the insides of 5 small baking molds. Divide mixture evenly among molds. Bake for 5 to 6 minutes. The center will be cooked but still runny. To serve, immediately invert molds on small plates. Top with powdered sugar and Grey Goose La Vanille crème anglaise.

Serves 5

ingredients

4 large Comice pears
1 lemon
2 tablespoons superfine sugar
6 tablespoons Grey Goose
   Le Citron
1 pinch ground nutmeg or
   freshly grated nutmeg
   sprig of fresh sage

Found at boutique produce stores, the Comice pear maintains its firmness even when ripe. The subtle honey taste of the pear would be perfect with your favorite Grey Goose martini.

grey goose le citron

comice pear

Preparation

Cut each pear into 6 sections, and remove the seeds. Divide the sections on 4 serving plates. Squeeze the lemon and sprinkle the juice on the pears. Mix the sugar and Grey Goose Le Citron.

Pour over the pears and refrigerate until ready to serve. To serve, sprinkle with nutmeg and garnish with a sprig of sage.

Serves 4

Lightly accented with Grey Goose L'Orange, this charming, citrus-toned crepe is appropriate for any occasion.

ingredients

crêpe batter
1 cup flour
¼ cup sugar
 pinch of salt
2 eggs
1 cup whole milk
1 tablespoon Grey Goose L'Orange

suzette butter
4 tablespoons soft, unsalted butter
 zest of 1 orange
¾ cup fresh squeezed orange juice
¼ cup Grey Goose L'Orange

garnish
¼ cup candied orange peel

grey goose l'orange

crêpes suzette

Crêpe batter
Combine the flour, sugar, salt, and eggs. Gradually stir in the milk and Grey Goose L'Orange until batter is smooth. Set aside for 1 hour at room temperature. Lightly oil an 8-inch sauté pan. When hot, pour in about ¼ cup batter. Swirl pan to completely coat the bottom, making a thin pancake. When lightly browned on bottom, turn over to lightly brown other side. Stack crêpes on a platter and cover with plastic wrap until ready to serve.

Suzette butter
In a large sauté pan, combine all the ingredients and bring to a boil. Fold crêpes into quarters and place in pan. To serve, place 2 or 3 hot crêpes on a plate. Spoon sauce over the crêpes and garnish with the candied orange peel.

Serves 4

ingredients

1½ cups graham cracker
   crumbs
3 tablespoons sugar
4 tablespoons unsalted butter,
   melted
5 eggs, separated
1 14-oz. can sweetened
   condensed milk
½ cup key lime juice
3 tablespoons Grey Goose
   Le Citron
½ teaspoon cream of tartar
⅓ cup sugar
   strips of lime peel for
   garnish

strawberry sauce

1 cup strawberry purée,
   strained
1 tablespoon fine sugar
4 tablespoons Grey Goose
   Le Citron

Marian Frank developed a love for this rich dessert while living in Palm Beach. A generous portion of Grey Goose Le Citron adds a distinct character to both the key lime pie and the accompanying strawberry sauce.

grey goose le citron
key lime pie

Crust
Preheat oven to 325°F. In a mixing bowl, stir together the graham cracker crumbs, 3 tablespoons sugar, and the melted butter. Press the crumb mixture into 6 greased 4-inch tartlet pan with a removable bottom and bake for 10 minutes. Remove from oven and let cool.

Filling
In a bowl, beat the egg yolks. Add the condensed milk, key lime juice, and Grey Goose Le Citron, and blend together. Pour the filling into the crusts and bake for 20 minutes or until set in the center. In a mixing bowl, beat the egg whites and cream of tartar until frothy. Add ⅓ cup sugar and beat until soft peaks form. Remove pies from oven. Increase oven temperature to 350°F. Gently spread the meringue over the pies and bake again until light golden in color. Transfer the pies to a wire rack to cool. Chill for at least 3 hours in the refrigerator.

Strawberry sauce
Mix all ingredients and serve cold.

Presentation
Gently pour strawberry sauce on the plates and place a pie in the center of each plate. Garnish the top with lime peel.

Serves 6

Chocolate lovers will delight in this fabulous combination of citrus and rich dark chocolate. Complement this delicious dessert with a Grey Goose La Vanille or L'Orange martini.

ingredients

7 ounces dark chocolate
7 tablespoons unsalted butter
6 egg whites, divided
3 egg yolks
  zest of 1 orange
4 tablespoons Grey Goose
  L'Orange
¼ teaspoon cream of tartar
¼ cup sugar

garnish
chocolate shavings or
  chips
orange zest juliennes

grey goose l'orange

mousse au chocolat

Preparation

Melt the chocolate and butter together in a microwave oven or bain-marie. Stir in 3 egg yolks, the orange zest, and Grey Goose L'Orange. Cool to room temperature. Beat 6 egg whites with the cream of tartar until stiff, then beat in the sugar. Gently fold the egg whites into the chocolate mixture until completely mixed. Pour into individual serving glasses or bowls. Garnish with chocolate shavings or chips and orange juliennes.

Serves 4

ingredients

- 8 large navel oranges
- 2 tablespoons superfine sugar
- 6 tablespoons Grey Goose L'Orange
- 1 pinch ground cinnamon
  fresh mint leaves

This is one of Sidney Frank's favorite desserts. He often has it as an afternoon snack or with Grey Goose L'Orange tea cake.

grey goose l'orange
orange salad

Preparation

Peel the oranges and remove the segments. Place the remaining part of the orange in a strainer over a bowl and press out any remaining juice. Mix the sugar and Grey Goose L'Orange, then add orange segments. Refrigerate until ready to serve.

To serve

Place the oranges with the juice in a serving bowl. Sprinkle with cinnamon and garnish with mint leaves. This summer dessert is best served cold along with Grey Goose L'Orange tea cake (see page 117).

Serves 4

Grey Goose L'Orange heightens the texture and palate of this dessert which is artfully served in frozen orange shells.

ingredients

- 4 navel oranges
- 4 cups fresh orange juice
- 1½ cups sugar
- 3 tablespoons corn syrup
- ⅓ cup orange pulp, finely chopped
- 4 tablespoons Grey Goose L'Orange

grey goose l'orange

sorbet

Preparation

Cut the top third off each orange and a small slice off the bottom to make it stand upright. Scoop out the pulp, and reserve the shell to fill with sorbet. Place shells in the freezer until ready to use. In a saucepan, combine 2 cups of orange juice, sugar, corn syrup, and orange pulp. Cook for about 4 minutes over medium heat or until the sugar has dissolved. Pour into a bowl; add remaining orange juice and Grey Goose L'Orange. Refrigerate for about 1 hour. Transfer the sorbet mixture to an ice cream maker and freeze according to the manufacturer's directions. Spoon sorbet into frozen shells. Freeze remaining sorbet in a covered container. Freeze all until ready to serve. Top shells with small scoops of remaining sorbet.

Serves 4

ingredients

- 9 tablespoons unsalted butter
- 1 pinch salt
- $1/2$ cup sugar
- 3 eggs
- 2 cups flour
- 2 teaspoons baking powder
- zest of 1 orange
- $1/4$ cup Grey Goose L'Orange

A delightful companion to either coffee or tea, this cake can be enjoyed at breakfast, tea time, or after dinner. Grey Goose L'Orange and orange zest impart a distinct citrus flavor.

grey goose l'orange
tea cake

Preparation

Preheat oven to 375°F. Butter a loaf pan and line the bottom with buttered wax paper. Cream the butter, salt, and sugar until yellow. Beat in the eggs one at a time. Mix in the flour, baking powder, orange zest, and Grey Goose L'Orange. Pour batter into prepared loaf pan. Bake in preheated oven for about 40 minutes or until golden brown.

Serves 6

This simple dessert combines several of Sidney Frank's favorite vices- ice cream, chocolate and, of course Grey Goose La Vanille. For a sophisticated combination, serve with Grey Goose La Vanille chocatinis.

ingredients

ice cream
3 cups whole milk
1 cup heavy cream
1 vanilla bean
$^1/_2$ cup sugar
6 egg yolks
1 tablespoon vanilla extract
$^1/_4$ cup Grey Goose La Vanille

sauce
$^1/_2$ cup semi-sweet chocolate
$^1/_4$ cup water
3 tablespoons Grey Goose La Vanille

garnish
small meringue cookies

grey goose la vanille

vanilla ice cream

Ice Cream
Prepare this recipe at least 4 hours in advance. It can be stored for up to 3 days before serving. In a large saucepan bring the milk, cream, vanilla bean and sugar to a boil over medium heat. Remove the vanilla bean, split the pod and scrape the seeds into the milk. Place the egg yolks in a mixing bowl and beat in 1 cup of hot milk. Add the vanilla extract and return the mixture to the saucepan. Whisk rapidly over medium-high heat for a few seconds. Do not boil. Remove the pan from the heat. The sauce should coat the back of the spoon. If the sauce is too thin, return the pan to the heat and whisk a few more seconds. Strain into a bowl, add Grey Goose La Vanille vodka and allow to cool. Transfer the ice cream mixture to an ice cream maker and freeze according to the manufacturer's directions.

Sauce
In a small saucepan over low heat, melt together the chocolate and water. Stir to mix well. Stir in the Grey Goose La Vanille vodka and simmer for 1 minute. If the sauce is too thin, cook it a few minutes longer. Remove the sauce from the heat and cool to room temperature. To serve, pour over Grey Goose La Vanille ice cream and garnish with small meringue cookies.

Serves 6

ingredients

- 1 pineapple
- 3 tablespoons Grey Goose La Vanille
- 1/3 cup brown sugar
- 1 teaspoon cinnamon
- 1/4 teaspoon allspice
- 1/4 teaspoon ground cloves
  freshly grated nutmeg for garnish

This refreshing tropical treat is a sweet finish to a barbecue or other summer feast.

grey goose la vanille

grilled pineapple

Preparation

Preheat the grill to medium temperature. Cut the pineapple lengthwise into 4 sections and keep the leaves intact. Sprinkle the Grey Goose La Vanille vodka evenly over the fruit. In a bowl, combine the sugar and spices and sprinkle the mixture over the wedges. Wrap the leaves with foil to keep the color. Place the wedges on the grill or in a preheated 400°F oven for 15 minutes and cook until the pineapple wedges have caramelized. To serve, place a pineapple wedge on each plate and grate fresh nutmeg on top for garnish.

Serves 4

This luscious vanilla custard stands up to the great crème brulees of the world.

ingredients

4 cups whole milk
²/₃ cup sugar
1 vanilla bean, cut in half
5 eggs
¼ cup Grey Goose La Vanille

caramel
½ cup sugar
¼ cup water
unsalted butter

grey goose la vanille

crème caramel

Caramel

In a small pan, stir in the sugar and water over medium-high heat until the sugar turns amber in color, about 10 minutes. Do not stir. Pour the caramel into 8 buttered molds.

Custard

Preheat oven to 350°F. In a pan over medium heat, bring the milk, sugar and vanilla bean to a boil. In a bowl, whip the eggs and add Grey Goose La Vanille vodka. Add the sugared milk to the bowl slowly, whipping quickly so that the eggs do not cook. Strain the mixture and take out the vanilla bean. Add the custard to the molds. Place the molds in a large pan. Add hot water to the pan halfway up the side of the molds. Bake for 30 minutes until set. Flip the molds over onto serving dish and serve cold.

Serves 8

ingredients

1   cup brown sugar
8   tablespoons unsalted butter
¼   coconut cream
1   pinch grated nutmeg
4   cinnamon sticks
6   bananas, sliced in half
½   cup Grey Goose La Vanille
      Grey Goose La Vanille
        ice cream (see page 118)

Ripe with citrus, sugar, and spices, this stunning dessert is surprisingly simple to prepare. Pair it with Grey Goose La Vanille Ice Cream for a mouth-watering finish to any meal.

grey goose la vanille
bananas flambées

Preparation

In a large frying pan, over medium heat, mix together the brown sugar, butter, coconut cream, grated nutmeg and cinnamon sticks. Reduce to low heat and cook until the sugar dissolves. Place the bananas in the pan and baste with the sauce. Cook over low heat until tender, but not soggy.

To flame

Pour Grey Goose La Vanille into the pan and bring to a boil. Remove from heat. Keeping your face well away from the pan, carefully ignite the vodka by touching a match to the pan's edge. Baste the bananas until the flames die. Transfer to serving plates and serve with Grey Goose La Vanille ice cream.

Serves 4

glossary

al dente: Italian for "to the tooth" and used to describe a food—usually pasta—that is cooked only until it gives a slight resistance when one bites into it; the food is neither soft nor overdone.

bain-marie: A hot water bath used to cook foods gently or to keep cooked foods hot; also known as a water bath.

baste: To moisten foods during cooking with melted fat, pan drippings, a sauce or other liquids to prevent drying and to add flavor.

blini: Hailing from Russia, blini are small, yeast-raised buckwheat pancakes traditionally served with sour cream and caviar or smoked salmon.

ceviche: A Latin American dish of raw fish marinated in citrus juice, onions, tomatoes and chiles and sometimes flavored with cilantro.

chanterelle: A trumpet-shaped wild mushroom found in North America and Europe; it has a ruffled-edge cap, a yellow-orange color, a smooth, slightly chewy texture, a distinctive fruity, nutty flavor and a clean, earthy aroma.

crème fraîche: A cultured cream product with a tart, tangy flavor similar to sour cream but thinner and richer.

crouton: A small piece of bread, often seasoned, that has been toasted, grilled or fried; it is used as a garnish for soup or salads.

foie gras: The enlarged liver of a duck or goose; it has two smooth, rounded lobes with a putty color and an extremely high fat content.

glace de canard: See glace de viande, but made from duck stock.

glace de viande: A dark brown, syrupy glaze made by reducing a brown stock; used to color and flavor sauces.

julienne:
1. Foods cut into a match stick shape of approximately $1/8$ x $1/8$ x $1/2$.
2. A garnish of foods cut in such a shape.

mousse: A French term meaning "froth" or "foam," mousse is a rich, airy dish that can be either sweet or savory and hot or cold. Cold dessert mousses are usually made with fruit purée or a flavoring such as chocolate. Their fluffiness is due to the addition of whipped cream or beaten egg whites and they're often fortified with gelatin. Hot mousses usually get their light texture from the addition of beaten egg whites.

mozzarella:
A southern Italian pasta filata cheese, originally made from water buffalo's milk but now also from cow's milk; it has a white color and a mild, delicate flavor used mostly for cooking.

purée: v. To process food to achieve a smooth pulp. n. A food that has been processed by mashing, straining or fine chopping to achieve a smooth pulp.

Roquefort: A semi-soft to hard french cheese made from ewe's milk; it has a creamy white interior with blue veins and a pungent, somewhat salty flavor; considered the prototype of blue chesses, true Roquefort, produced only in Roquefort, France, is authenticated by a red sheep on the wrapper and contains approximately 45% milk fat.

salmon caviar: Roe harvested from chum and silver salmon; the large eggs have an orange color and a good flavor.

sautéing: A dry-heat cooking method that uses conduction to transfer heat from a hot pan to food with the aid of a small amount of fat; cooking is usually done quickly over high temperatures.

tapenade: A thick paste made from capers, anchovies, olives, olive oil, lemon juice and seasonings in France's Provence region; used as a condiment, garnish and sauce.

tartare: An imprecisely used term for any dish featuring a raw ingredient.

white truffle: A truffle grown in Italy with an off-white to grayish-tan skin and an earthy, garlicky flavor; also known as piédmontese.

zest: v. To remove strips of rind from a citrus fruit. n. The colored, outermost layer of a citrus rind; used for flavoring creams, custards and baked goods; it can be candied and used as a confection or decoration.

acknowledgments

Grand merci à Sidney Frank for giving the inspiration to write this book and the opportunity to cook with the Grey Goose Vodkas.

Marian Frank, I appreciate your friendship and your willingness to sample my recipes and offer feedback.

I would like to give a special thanks to Cathy Halstead for her advice and support throughout the development of the book.

Also, I would like to acknowledge Lee Einsidler for having the foresight to endorse and to see the potential for the book from the beginning.

Thank you to Deirdre Maher and Aaron Crecy for lending writing support to the book.

I would like to thank Sarah Zeiler who has deftly helped to promote the cookbook.

Bill Henderson, Michael Bond, Jack Egan and iDesign who assisted with the layout of the book and pro-vided art direction throughout the project.

Thanks to everyone at Sidney Frank Importing Co. who helped to make this book possible.

Susan Draudt, who helped to style my dishes for the camera.

Michael Smith and Eddie Berman whose cameras so beautifully captured the images.

To Chino's Farm in Rancho Santa Fe, which features the finest and best tasting organic vegetables in California.

D'Artagnan in New Jersey, which supplies me with beautiful foie gras from France and marvelous poultry.

Special thanks to the team at Tehabi Books. It was a pleasure to work with each of these marvelous and gifted people during the course of this project.

Pascal Courtin

notes

notes

sidney frank

Sidney Frank is the founder and Chairman of Sidney Frank Importing Co., Inc., the American importer of such successful brands as Jägermeister Liqueur, Grey Goose Vodka, and Gekkeikan Saké.

Born in Norwich, Connecticut, Sidney attended Brown University before heading to Asia where he represented Pratt & Whitney Motors during World War II. Upon his return to the United States in 1945, Sidney found work with Schenley Distillers where he was responsible for the success of such brands as Dewar's White Label and Ancient Age.

In 1972, Sidney founded Sidney Frank Importing Co., Inc. His reputation as a brand builder has won him such brands as Jägermeister Liqueur, which he built into the third best-selling imported liqueur in the United States.

In 1997, Sidney developed Grey Goose Vodka from France. Winner of the Beverage Testing Institute's Platinum Medal, Grey Goose Vodka has been named the "World's Best Tasting Vodka." Sidney has followed this success with the introductions of Grey Goose L'Orange, Grey Goose Le Citron, Grey Goose La Vanille, and is currently at work on new products.

Active in various professional, cultural, and charitable organizations, Sidney is Chairman of the Board of the Sidney and Louise Frank Foundation and is a Board Member of the Riverdale Country School where he has established scholarships for Scholar-Athletes. An avid golfer and art collector, Sidney and his wife, Marian, live in New Rochelle, New York. Sidney has two children and five grandchildren.

chef pascal courtin

Specializing in French and international cuisine, Pascal Courtin is the personal chef for Sidney Frank, the founder and Chairman of Sidney Frank Importing Co., Inc.

Pascal was born in 1967 in the heart of Bordeaux, France's fabled wine region. After earning several certifications in gastronomy and restaurant management from the Culinary School of Bordeaux and certification in oenology from La Tour Blanche, Pascal trained extensively at Claude Darroze, the celebrated restaurant which boasts a one-star Michelin rating.

An acclaimed gourmet chef and pastry artist, Pascal has served in executive posts for a number of renowned restaurants and dignitaries. He achieved particular distinction while in the private employ of the artist, le Baron Alain de Condé. The last of a line of the royal Condé family of France, le Baron has long been a fixture in Bordeaux society and is one of its most celebrated hosts. During that appointment, Pascal had the pleasure to serve a colorful list of luminaries including la Baronne Nadine de Rothschild, Maurice Druon, and Hubert de Givenchy.

Today, Pascal travels with Sidney Frank and devotes much of his time to dreaming up new recipes using the Sidney Frank Importing brands.

index